The Palace

I used to turn my back to friends, if their religion was not similar to mine.
Now, my heart has become capable of every form:

It is a pasture for gazelles,
And a convent for Christian monks,
And a temple for idols and the pilgrim's Kaaba,
And the scrolls of the Torah, and the book of the Qur'an.

I follow the religion of love wherever its ships might sail,
for love is my religion and creed.

➤➤ IBN AL-ARABI, ANDALUSIAN MYSTIC AND POET

LIFE IN
THE MEDIEVAL MUSLIM WORLD

The Palace

KATHRYN HINDS

MARSHALL CAVENDISH BENCHMARK NEW YORK

In memory of Serena Wilson

The author and publishers wish to extend heartfelt thanks to Dr. Josef W. Meri, Fellow and Special Scholar in Residence, Royal Aal al-Bayt Institute for Islamic Thought, Amman, Jordan, for his gracious and invaluable assistance in reviewing the manuscript.

MARSHALL CAVENDISH BENCHMARK 99 WHITE PLAINS ROAD TARRYTOWN, NEW YORK 10591 www.marshallcavendish.us Text copyright © 2009 by Marshall Cavendish Corporation. Map copyright © 2009 by Mike Reagan. All rights reserved. No part of this book may be reproduced or utilized in any form or by any means electronic or mechanical including photocopying, recording, or by any information storage and retrieval system, without permission from the copyright holders. All Internet sites were available and accurate when this book was sent to press. LIBRARY OF CONGRESS CATALOGING-IN-PUBLICATION DATA Hinds, Kathryn, 1962- The palace / by Kathryn Hinds. p. cm. — (Life in the medieval Muslim world) Includes bibliographical references and index. Summary: "A social history of the Islamic world from the eighth through the mid-thirteenth century, with a focus on life in the upper echelons of society"—Provided by publisher. ISBN 978-0-7614-3088-9 1. Islamic Empire—History—750-1258. 2. Elite (Social sciences)—Islamic Empire. 3. Islamic Empire—Social life and customs. 4. Islamic Empire—Social conditions. I. Title. DS38.6.H65 2009 909'.1—dc22 2008010734

EDITOR: Joyce Needleman Stanton   PUBLISHER: Michelle Bisson
ART DIRECTOR: Anahid Hamparian   SERIES DESIGNER: Kristen Branch / MichaelNelsonDesign

Images provided by Rose Corbett Gordon and Alexandra (Sasha) Gordon, Art Editors of Mystic CT, from the following sources: Cover: Mary Evans Picture Library/The Image Works Back cover: Werner Forman Archive/Art Resource, NY Page 1: National Museum, New Delhi, Delhi, India/Borromeo/Art Resource, NY; pages 2-3: Archivo Iconografico/Corbis; page 6: Bildarchiv Steffens/Bridgeman Art Library; pages 8, 55: The Gallery Collection/Corbis; pages 9, 68: Bridgeman-Giraudon/Art Resource, NY; page 11: The Metropolitan Museum of Art/Art Resource, NY; page 12: The Art Archive/Galleria degli Uffizi Florence/Alfredo Dagli Orti; page 15: Carmen Redondo/Corbis; page 16: Snark/Art Resource, NY; page 17: Arthur M. Sackler Gallery, Smithsonian Institution, Washington. D.C., Purchase—Smithsonian Unrestricted Trust Funds, Smithsonian Collections Acquisition Program, and Dr. Arthur Sackler, S1986.175a; page 19: Private Collection, Giraudon/Bridgeman Art Library; pages 22, 66: Werner Forman/Topham/The Image Works; page 25: The Art Archive/Gianni Dagli Orti; page 28: The Art Archive/Manuel Cohen; page 29: Michael Busselle/Corbis; page 31: The Art Archive/Turkish and Islamic Art Museum Istanbul/Alfredo Dagli Orti; page 32: Adam Woolfitt/Corbis; page 34: Freer Gallery of Art, Smithsonian Institution, Washington, D.C., Purchase F1930.71; page 36: National Gallery Collection, by kind permission of the Trustees of the National Gallery, London/Corbis; pages 40, 79: The Art Archive/Musée Condé Chantilly/Gianni Dagli Orti; page 43: The Art Archive/National Museum Damascus Syria/Gianni Dagli Orti; page 45: The Art Archive/Corbis; pages 47, 48, 49: Bettmann/Corbis; page 50: Borromeo/Art Resource, NY; page 53: The Image Works; page 57: Musee d'Orsay, Paris,Lauros/Giraudon/Bridgeman Art Library; page 59: The Art Archive/Musée du Louvre Paris/Gianni Dagli Orti; page 60: The Art Archive/British Library/Eileen Tweedy; page 63: The Art Archive/Bodleian Library Oxford; page 65: The Art Archive/National Museum Damascus Syria/Gianni Dagli Orti; page 70: The British Library/HIP/The Image Works; page 72: Roger-Viollet/The Image Works; page 75: The Art Archive/National Library Cairo/Gianni Dagli Orti; pages 76, 81: The Art Archive/Museum of Islamic Art Cairo/Gianni Dagli Orti; page 80: The Art Archive/Real Biblioteca de El Escorial/Gianni Dagli Orti; page 83: The Art Archive/British Library.

Printed in China
135642

front cover: A courtyard in the Alhambra, one of the palaces of Muslim Spain
half-title page: A gazelle pictured in a manuscript from Muslim-ruled northern India
title page: Christian ambassadors are presented to the caliph of Córdoba as the scientists of his court pursue their studies.
back cover: A gazelle decorates a pottery bowl from eleventh-century North Africa.

Contents

The angel Gabriel brings divine revelation to Muhammad. So that viewers will not be tempted to worship his image, the Prophet is shown with his face veiled.

About the
Medieval Muslim World

IN THE YEAR 622 AN ARABIAN MERCHANT NAMED Muhammad, accompanied by two hundred followers, left his home city of Mecca for the troubled town of Yathrib. Its citizens knew that Muhammad had been receiving visions from God and preaching what God had revealed to him. His message was unpopular in Mecca, but the people of Yathrib welcomed Muhammad to be their chief judge and embraced his teaching of Islam, or submission to God. They recognized Muhammad as the Prophet of God, and their city soon became known as Madinat al-Nabi, "City of the Prophet," or simply Medina.

The Hegira, Muhammad's move to Medina, marked the beginning of the Islamic community, the *umma*. From that point on, the community of Muslims (followers of Islam) grew rapidly. By 634 it embraced the entire Arabian Peninsula. By 750 Muslim rulers controlled a wide band of territory from the Iberian Peninsula, across North Africa, to the borders of India. During the following centuries the *umma* continued to expand into India, Anatolia (modern Turkey), central Asia, and sub-Saharan Africa. Along the way, Arab and local cultures mingled and sometimes melded,

This page from a Qur'an copied out in the ninth century shows the care and artistry used to pass on the holy words.

leading to the development of a shared Muslim culture with many ways of expressing itself.

The Dar al-Islam, "Abode of Islam," was politically united for only a brief period. But it remained united in other important ways, through religious beliefs and language. Arabic, the language of the Qur'an (the holy book of Islam), became the common tongue of nearly all Muslims in Islam's early centuries. In most areas it was used not just in religion but also in government, law, literature, and learning. This meant that no matter where a Muslim went in the Dar al-Islam, he or she would be able to share news and knowledge with other Muslims. In fact the gathering, communication, and spreading of knowledge and skills in the arts and sciences was one of the great achievements of the Muslim world during this era. For this reason, it is often referred to as the Golden Age of Islam. In the history of the West, this time is generally called the Middle Ages, and for convenience we use both that term and *medieval* for this period even when discussing areas outside Europe.

The Dar al-Islam and Christian medieval Europe often conflicted with each other. Yet there was also a great deal of peaceful interchange between the two, in many ways to the lasting benefit of European civilization. And at various times and places in the

The Palace

8

A page from a book by the great scholar Moses Maimonides, a leader of the Jewish community in Egypt

medieval Muslim world, Muslims, Christians, and Jews lived and worked side by side in an atmosphere of tolerance seldom found elsewhere in the past. In the present, too, we can find much to learn from both the successes and the struggles of the Dar al-Islam in the Middle Ages.

About the Medieval Muslim World

This series of books looks at the lives of the people who lived in that diverse world, focusing mainly on the Middle East and Spain in the eighth through thirteenth centuries. In this volume we will meet the people at the highest level of society: the rulers, government officials, and courtiers, and their wives and children. We will visit their palaces and enjoy some of the beauty and poetry that surrounded them. We will see what kinds of work they did, how they relaxed, and how they coped with life's hardships. So step back into history, to a time of faith and intellect, intrigue and excitement, struggle and splendor. Welcome to life in the medieval Muslim world!

A Note on Dates and Names

For Muslims the Hegira (Arabic *hijra*, "departure" or "emigration") began a new age and so became the year 1 of the Muslim calendar. Dates in this calendar are labeled AH, for *Anno Hegira*, or simply H. For ease of reading, though, this series of books uses the conventional Western dating system. Also for ease of reading, we are using the common Westernized forms of many Arabic names—for example, *Avicenna* instead of *Ibn Sina*—and we are leaving out most of the special accent marks that scholars use when converting Arabic names to the Western alphabet. There are many different ways to convert Arabic to English, especially because the Arabic alphabet does not include symbols for vowels. For this reason, you may see the same names spelled in slightly different ways in different books. In many sources you may also see the God of Islam referred to as Allah. Since the Arabic word *Allah* simply means *God* and refers to the same deity worshipped by Jews and Christians, we have chosen to use *God* instead of *Allah* in this series.

Above: Elegant Arabic script decorates this glass lamp from the 1200s.
The lamp helped light a Cairo mosque and also symbolized the light of God.

Saladin, the twelfth-
century sultan of
Egypt and Syria, as
imagined by a
sixteenth-century
Italian artist

ONE

Caliphs, Emirs, and Sultans

In every age and time God (be He exalted) chooses one member of the human
race and, having adorned and endowed him with kingly virtues, entrusts him
with the interests of the world and the well–being of His servants.

→→ Nizam al–Mulk, eleventh–century vizier to Sultan Malik–Shah

URING HIS LIFETIME, MUHAMMAD GOVERNED the Muslim community as both its religious and political leader. When he died in 632, the group of men closest to him chose his friend and father-in-law, Abu Bakr, to take his place as leader. Unlike Muhammad, Abu Bakr was not regarded as a prophet. Instead, he was the Prophet's caliph (*khalifa* in Arabic)— his deputy or successor. This title was passed on to those who followed Abu Bakr, and for centuries the caliph reigned as the political and spiritual head of the *umma*. As time went on, his role became mainly symbolic, but during Islam's early years his power was very real indeed.

13

The first four of Muhammad's successors were known as the Rightly Guided Caliphs, and their seat of government was in Medina. The last of these caliphs was the Prophet's son-in-law, Ali. When he was murdered in 661, the governor of Syria, Mu'awiya, claimed the caliphate. Mu'awiya was a strong military commander and a crafty politician and diplomat. He had been one of Muhammad's secretaries as well as his brother-in-law, and he was also the cousin of the third of the Rightly Guided Caliphs, Uthman.

By the time Mu'awiya came to power, the Dar al-Islam encompassed land from Egypt east to Persia and from Arabia north to Armenia. Much of this land had been won from the Greek Byzantine Empire (in the west) and the Persian Sasanian Empire (in the east). To better control all this territory, Mu'awiya moved the capital from Medina up to Damascus, Syria. In addition this placed him in a stronger position to fight the Byzantines, who still held Anatolia and wanted to reclaim the lands they had lost.

Mu'awiya also changed the way caliphs were chosen. Previously they had been selected by a small committee of Medina's leading citizens. But Mu'awiya nominated one of his sons to succeed him, and afterward hereditary rule became standard practice. The series of rulers that began with Mu'awiya came to be known as the Umayyad dynasty, from Mu'awiya and Uthman's ancestor Umayya.

The Umayyads stretched the boundaries of the Dar al-Islam westward to what are now Spain and Portugal, and eastward to what are now Uzbekistan and Pakistan. The Muslim armies did not, however, try to convert the conquered peoples to Islam. For one thing, the defeated non-Muslims paid the taxes that supported the Umayyad government. In fact, people who wanted to convert were usually turned away. At this time, Islam was still closely identified

with the Arabians and their military elite—and many wanted to keep it that way. The Muslim armies occupying conquered territories lived in and controlled things from garrison cities. Most Muslims mixed with few local people other than the prisoners-of-war who became their household slaves.

By around 700 this situation was changing. Muslim soldiers were acquiring land and leaving the garrisons to farm it. Villagers moved to the garrison cities and converted to Islam. The Umayyad caliphs recruited more and more soldiers from outside Arabia, who also converted. Provincial governors had already been using local people as tax collectors and administrators, and soon non-Arabians (and even non-Muslims) would begin to occupy higher offices in government. Through these and similar processes, more people embraced Islam, and social and cultural diversity increased throughout the Muslim world.

The Umayyad caliph al-Walid ordered the construction of a splendid mosque in Damascus. He hired Greek craftsmen to decorate it with elaborate mosaics such as this one. It may have been intended to depict the beauties of Paradise.

THE HIGH POINT OF THE CALIPHATE

The Umayyads were overthrown in 750 by the Abbasids, who took their name from the Prophet's uncle al-Abbas, their ancestor. The

Harun ar-Rashid as a young man armed to go hunting, from a seventeenth-century Indian edition of *The Thousand and One Nights*

bulk of the early Abbasids' military force came from northeastern Persia, and the influence of Persian culture soon became strong in the court of the caliphs. Under the second Abbasid caliph, al-Mansur, the court moved east to the newly founded city of Baghdad in Iraq. Here the caliphs fostered an atmosphere where poetry, music, art and architecture, philosophy, science, and scholarship flourished. They also established a strong, centralized system of government that made their power unrivaled for more than a hundred years.

The most famous of the Abbasid caliphs is Harun ar-Rashid, who became a figure of folklore and legend in the stories known as *The Arabian Nights* or *The Thousand and One Nights*. There were two important symbols of the caliph's leadership of the *umma*, and Harun pursued both vigorously. The first was leading the pilgrimage to the holy city of Mecca, which Harun did eight times during his reign. The second was the waging of holy war. Nearly every year he sent an expedition against the Byzantines, often leading the army in person. He also reformed the system of taxation in the outlying provinces to raise more money for this warfare.

Harun was followed as caliph by his three sons in succession. The third son, al-Mu'tasim, was not a lover of arts and literature like his father and brothers. He preferred outdoor pursuits and military matters. Determined to reform the army to his own design, he bought thousands of Turkish slaves, young men or boys from Central Asia. After they converted to Islam they were freed, but as

In Praise of Turkish Horsemen

Al-Mu'tasim's elite corps of Turkish slave-soldiers in the 830s was a subject of great controversy. Many citizens of Baghdad—especially members of the military—complained bitterly about it. To others, though, the advantages were clear, as court-favored essayist al-Jahiz explained:

The Turk will hit from his saddle an animal, a bird, a target, a man, a couching animal, a marker post or a bird of prey stooping on its quarry. His horse may be exhausted from being galloped and reined in, wheeled to right and left, and mounted and dismounted: but he himself goes on shooting, loosing ten arrows before [his enemy] has let fly one. . . . Especially formidable is his trick of using his lasso to throw a horse and unseat its rider, all at full gallop. . . . [The Turks] train their horsemen to carry two or even three bows, and spare bowstrings in proportion. Thus in the hour of battle the Turk has on him everything needful for himself, his weapon and the care of his steed. As for their ability to stand trotting, sustained galloping, long rides and cross-country journeys, it is truly extraordinary. . . . If the [Turk's] daily life were to be reckoned up in detail, he would be found to spend more time in the saddle than on the ground.

Above: With their skills in archery and horsemanship,
Turkish warriors came to play more and more important roles in Muslim armies.

both slaves and freedmen they were loyal only to their master. As foreigners, they had no interest in local feuds or politics. Best of all, as mounted archers they had military skills unequaled by any other soldiers in the Dar al-Islam. Al-Mu'tasim couldn't foresee it, but from this point on, Turkish soldiers would become important figures at court and Turkish peoples would play an ever greater role in the affairs of the medieval Muslim world.

COMMANDERS AND KINGS

One of the titles borne by the caliphs was *amir al-mu'minin*, "commander of the faithful." The plain title *amir*, or emir as it is usually spelled in English, came to be used for military commanders and governors under the caliphs' authority. A royal prince might also be called an emir. One such prince was Abd ar-Rahman I, a member of the Umayyad family who had escaped Damascus when the Abbasids took over.

By 756 Abd ar-Rahman had reached Spain and defeated the feuding Muslim forces that had occupied most of the Iberian Peninsula since 711. He took control of al-Andalus (the Arabic name for Muslim Spain) as emir, giving token respect to the caliph, and made his capital at Córdoba. He was a strong ruler and set al-Andalus on a course of power and prosperity. The sixteenth-century North African historian al-Maqqari noted that even though Abd ar-Rahman "could only see out of one eye, and was destitute of the sense of smelling," his appearance "inspired with awe all those who approached him."

Al-Andalus became so powerful that in 929 Abd ar-Rahman III took the title *caliph*, proclaiming himself and his realm completely independent of the Baghdad caliphate. Other Muslim leaders also broke away from Baghdad, especially after 945, when the Buyid dynasty of warlords from Persia conquered Iraq and reduced the Abbasid caliph to a mere figurehead. "Prophecy and the caliphate

Strong rulers in various parts of the *umma* were able to break away from the caliphate in Baghdad. Eventually the Abbasid caliph would become little more than a figurehead.

belong to the Arabs, but kingship belongs to the Persians" became a popular saying.

The Dar al-Islam was no longer a single political unit. There had always been some areas where the caliphs had minimal control, provinces that at times were practically self-ruling in all but name. Some Muslim states didn't even pretend loyalty to the Abbasids. The rulers of the North African Fatimid dynasty (named after the Prophet's daughter Fatima) had been calling themselves caliphs since 909. In 969 they took over Egypt and established their new city of Cairo as the capital of their caliphate.

In 977 the Turkish dynasty known as the Ghaznavids (from the city of Ghazni, their base in Afghanistan) seized power in eastern Persia and began to extend their influence. By 1030, thanks especially to the wars conducted by Mahmud of Ghazni, the Ghaznavids controlled most of Persia, all of Afghanistan, and what are now Pakistan and northwestern India. Mahmud and the other Ghaznavids were careful to present themselves as subjects of the caliph, although in fact the caliph had no actual power over them. The Ghaznavids used the title emir, but they were also among the first to call themselves sultans.

Sultan was a word that occurred in the Qur'an and referred to worldly or political power (separate from authority over spiritual matters). Basically, a sultan was a king or absolute monarch. Other early users of this title were the Seljuk Turks. Originally from Central Asia east of the Aral Sea, they began to wrest power from the Ghaznavids and the Buyids. During the mid-1000s, they took over both Persia and Iraq. They went on to fight the Fatimids and the Byzantines, and by 1090 they ruled from central Anatolia to the border of China. An eleventh-century author, Mahmud of Kashgar, wrote, "I have seen that God has caused the sun of empire to rise in the house of the Turks."

Seljuk rule did not reach Egypt, which remained under the Fatimids. But in 1169 the Kurdish general Salah ad-Din Yusuf ibn Ayyub, or Saladin, became vizier to the Fatimid caliph. Two years later, as the caliph lay dying, Saladin declared allegiance to the Abbasid caliph and named himself sultan of Egypt. He and his successors, the Ayyubids, ruled Egypt and much of Syria till 1250. In that year the last Ayyubid sultan was killed, the victim of a revolution by a group of Turkish soldiers who about a century before had been brought to Egypt as slaves. After rising to high army and government posts, the Mamluks, as they were called, seized power and started their own dynasty. It would last until 1517. The majority of the Dar al-Islam was now in Turkish hands.

The Palace

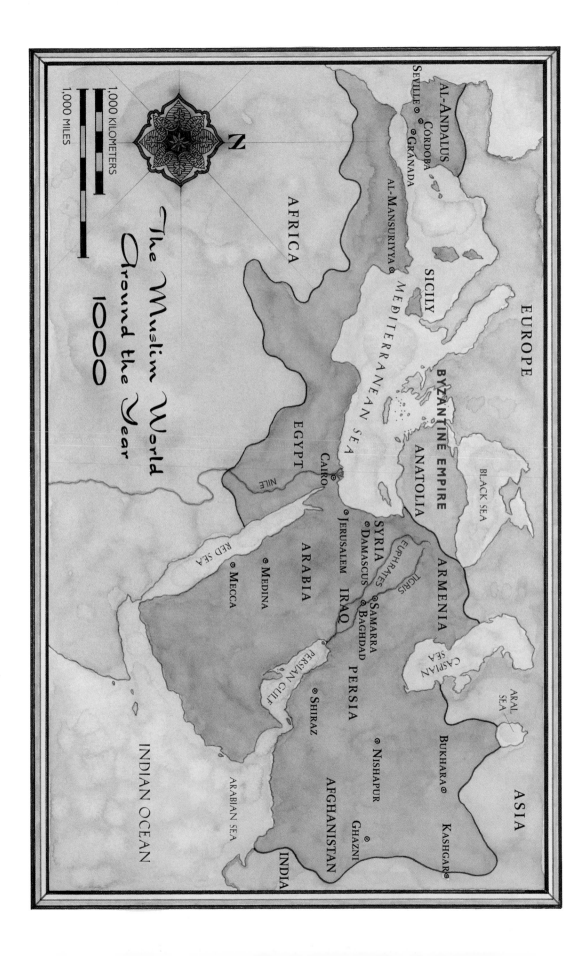

The Court of the Lions in the Alhambra, probably the most famous of all the palaces built in al-Andalus

TWO

Princely Palaces

I saw a series of buildings, terraces, rooms . . . there was a throne
in one of them that took up the entire width of the room.

→→NASR-I KHUSRAW, TWELFTH-CENTURY PERSIAN POET AND SCHOLAR

REGARDLESS OF HIS TITLE—CALIPH, EMIR, OR sultan—a ruler needed a place to live and a headquarters for his government. His palace was both. It was also a symbol of his wealth, strength, and authority. For this reason, rulers often were not content with the palaces of those who came before them. Wanting to outdo their forerunners, they made splendid additions to old palaces or built entirely new ones. Sometimes they felt the need to make an even stronger statement; this was especially true when a new dynasty came to power. As the essayist al-Jahiz commented, "Kings and princes are naturally inclined to efface [wipe out] the traces of their predecessors, so as to destroy the memory of their enemies."

War, the effects of passing time, modern development, and other forces have combined to leave few remains of the palaces of medieval Muslim rulers. Fortunately, however, we have still been able to learn much about them thanks to art, literature, and archaeology.

ABBASID POWER CENTERS

When the second Abbasid caliph, al-Mansur, decided to move his capital out of Syria, he ordered Baghdad to be built as a perfectly round city with his palace and the mosque at the center. Known as the Palace of the Golden Gate, al-Mansur's new home was topped by a green dome with a statue of a horseman on its peak; it could be seen from beyond the city limits. A tenth-century author wrote that the Palace of the Golden Gate "was the crown of Baghdad, a guidepost for the region and one of the great achievements of the Abbasids."

Nevertheless, al-Mansur later built another residence, the Eternity Palace, outside the city walls; the Palace of the Golden Gate became more of a government office building. Many other palaces were built in and around Baghdad by succeeding caliphs and members of the royal family. There were also palaces in other parts of Iraq and in eastern Syria that could function as royal hunting lodges and country retreats, regional administration centers, and bases for launching military campaigns against the Byzantines and other enemies.

These early Abbasid palaces had many things in common. They usually had only one floor, and the roofs were mainly flat. One of the central and most important rooms was the *iwan*, a large hall (often with a high, vaulted ceiling) open on one end; the opening might face a courtyard or another great hall. The *iwan* was where the caliph held court: hearing the complaints of his subjects, dis-

Al-Kazimain Mosque began as a cemetery established by Harun ar-Rashid on the outskirts of Baghdad. After a group of important religious leaders were buried there in the 800s, it became a holy place. The mosque's construction was begun in the eleventh century and finished in the nineteenth century.

pensing justice, receiving ambassadors, and so on. Every palace also had a mosque and a bathhouse. Other parts of the palace would include private quarters for the ruler and his family, guests, retainers, and servants. During this time period there was no harem, or enclosed area for the palace women. Royal women, however, often had their own palaces and households.

In 836 the caliph al-Mu'tasim moved the Abbasid capital from Baghdad north to his new city of Samarra, a better base for the Turkish troops he had recruited. He built on a grand scale, as did those who followed him (until the caliphate moved back to Baghdad in 892); eventually there were about thirty palaces in the city. The main Samarra palace complex covered more than 430 acres (six times larger than Baghdad's Palace of the Golden Gate). Beneath it, a tunnel network allowed palace personnel to ride donkeys from one part of the complex to another.

This palace was situated on a low bluff near the bank of the Tigris River. Visitors arrived by water and climbed a flight of marble steps to the Gate of the People, which led into the Public Palace. They passed through several halls and courtyards before reaching a domed room with an *iwan* on each of its four sides. Here they might have an audience with the caliph. An eleventh-century author described a Samarra throne room this way:

> The caliph Mutawwwakil [reigned 847–861] had it decorated with great images of gold and silver and made a great pool whose surfacing inside and out was in plates of silver. He put on it a tree made of gold in which birds twittered and whistled. He had a great throne made of gold on which there were two images of huge lions and the steps to it had images of lions and eagles and other things. . . . He sat in the palace on his golden throne, dressed in a robe of rich brocade and he ordered that all those who entered his presence should be dressed in finely woven brocades.

After the audience, some select visitors might continue on through more halls and courtyards, till they came to a grandstand that overlooked a racetrack. All these ceremonial halls and courtyards were located along the palace's east-west axis; on the north-south axis were found smaller rooms, most of them multipurpose, although one housed the caliph's treasury. The others could be used as sleeping quarters, sitting rooms, dining rooms, or storerooms, as needed.

Iraq had few stone quarries, so the palaces of Baghdad and Samarra were built mainly of kiln-baked bricks and adobe (sun-dried mud bricks). But at the other end of the Muslim world, in al-Andalus, stone was an abundant resource. There, a few miles northwest of Córdoba, some ten thousand laborers worked for twenty-five years cutting as many as six thousand stone blocks a day. The blocks were used to build the palace-city of Madinat al-Zahra, begun around 936 by Caliph Abd ar-Rahman III and finished by his son in 961. By this time it was home to around twelve thousand people.

Madinat al-Zahra was built on a high hill, terraced to make three levels. The lowest level was inhabited by soldiers, servants, laborers, and craftspeople; here, too, was a marketplace, mosque, and public bathhouses. Government officials lived and worked on the middle terrace. At the top was the caliph's residence, with its audience chambers and reception rooms. The palace incorporated 4,313 marble columns, many of them taken from ancient Roman ruins. One reception hall, according to al-Maqqari, "had eight openings formed by interlacing arches of ebony and ivory inlaid with gold and all manner of precious gems. . . . When the sun came through these openings and its rays rebounded off the roof and walls, the hall sparkled with light."

As in Samarra, visitors had to pass through many passageways and other chambers in order to come into the caliph's presence. And at least one foreign ambassador found that even before he reached the gate of al-Zahra, he had to walk up a road lined on both sides with soldiers, "with spears held erect, beside them others brandishing javelins and staging demonstrations of aiming them at each other." As the mystic and poet Ibn al-Arabi remarked

Elegant arches, patterned brick-work, sculpted plaster, and colorful marble columns still ornament the remains of a royal reception hall in Madinat al-Zahra.

of such displays, "The fear that this inspired was indescribable."

In 1013, after being sacked by North African invaders, Madinat al-Zahra fell into ruin. Córdoba was conquered in 1236 by the Christian king of Léon and Castile in northern Spain, and by 1250 only the city of Granada and its surrounding territory, in southern-most Spain, remained in Muslim hands. Overlooking Granada, the ruling Nasrid dynasty had a hilltop fortress nestled into the Sierra Nevada range. In the early 1300s the Nasrids began to turn the fortress into a palace complex, the Alhambra (from Arabic *al-hamra,* "the red," because of its red clay walls). By the 1370s there were six or seven palaces within the Alhambra's walls, along with gardens, mosques, bathhouses, soldiers' barracks, stables, the royal mint, a cemetery, and the homes and workshops of craftspeople and others who served the court. In all, about forty thousand people lived in

The Palace

the Alhambra. Today two of the Nasrids' Alhambra palaces still stand, among the world's architectural jewels. They give us a hint of the magnificence that must have surrounded the great dynasties and rulers of the medieval Muslim world.

The Alhambra is the only medieval Muslim palace still standing. In the days when it was home to the sultan of Granada, it was at least three times bigger than it is now.

EGYPT AND ELSEWHERE

One of the great powers of the medieval Middle East was the Fatimid dynasty, under which Egypt gained more wealth and prestige than it had enjoyed since the time of the pharaohs. When the Fatimid caliph al-Muizz settled in Cairo in 969, he immediately had a magnificent palace built, with a parade ground to the east. His successor built another palace on the other side of the parade ground, which became known as Bayn al-Qasrayn ("Between the Two Palaces")—still the name of a broad street running through the old section of Cairo.

By the 1200s the Fatimid palace had ten separate pavilions connected by underground passages. The caliphs filled the palace with valuables of all kinds—the royal treasury at one point contained not just gems and precious metals and antique rugs and the like, but also such things as an all-silver model of a garden and a golden, jewel-studded peacock. When the caliphs held audience, they used their wealth to create an opulent setting that would impress all those who came before them. The Persian poet Nasr-i Khusraw felt the full effect when he visited the palace in the 1100s; he left this description of the caliph's throne and its surroundings:

> Three of its sides were made of gold on which were hunting scenes depicting riders racing their horses, and other subjects; there were also inscriptions written in beautiful characters. The rugs and hangings were Greek satin . . . woven precisely to fit the spot where they were to be placed. A balustrade [low barrier] of golden lattice-work surrounded the throne, whose beauty defies description. Behind the throne were steps of silver. I saw a tree that looked like an orange tree, whose branches, leaves, and fruit were made of sugar. A thousand statuettes and figurines also made of sugar were placed there.

In Afghanistan, Sultan Mahmud of Ghazni had a similarly splendid throne, made of red gold. He sat under his crown, which hung from a chain over his head. It was so heavy, though, that it was also held up by the outstretched arms of four statues. The walls of the throne room were decorated with paintings of soldiers standing guard. In Persia and Iraq, the Seljuk sultans surrounded themselves not with paintings of soldiers but with life-size figures

This Persian scene of a ruler and his courtiers shows the opulent fabrics, woodwork, and metalwork that decorated palaces.

of guards and other palace attendants, made of carefully sculpted and painted plaster.

BEAUTY, LUXURY, AND COMFORT

A medieval Muslim ruler's palace was generally not a single building but a group of buildings, gardens, and courtyards. Sometimes their arrangement was very orderly; sometimes it was almost mazelike. When ambassadors from the Byzantine Empire came to Baghdad in 917, they were led all through the palace, including the stables and the compounds where the caliph's lions and elephants lived. In total, the ambassadors visited at least twenty-three different palace buildings before they finally came before the caliph.

Within each building of a medieval Muslim palace, most rooms were multipurpose and relatively small. Their magnificence came from the way they were decorated. A favorite form of ornamentation was stucco, sculpted plaster, used on walls, ceilings, and columns.

Ceramic tiles were used to beautify buildings through-out the Muslim world. Here they form part of the decoration on the walls of the royal baths of the Alhambra.

Wood paneling and carvings, too, were popular with many rulers. Sometimes walls were faced with marble; Mahmud of Ghazni's palace abounded in marble acquired during his wars in India. Wall paintings were also common in many palaces. Sometimes these and other decorations portrayed people, animals, plants, or signs of the zodiac; frequently they were abstract or geometrical designs, often of great complexity. Words, too, painted or carved in elegant calligraphy, could ornament many parts of a palace. The Alhambra is full of such texts—for example, this inscription on a courtyard wall: "The water in the basin [fountain] in my centre is like the soul of a believer who rests in the remembrance of God."

Texts and other decorations on palace walls were often not far above floor level, so that they could be seen and enjoyed from a seated position—royalty and courtiers alike typically sat (and slept) on cushions or rugs. Beautifully woven rugs and wall hangings, in rich colors and the finest fabrics, were among a ruler's most precious possessions. Rulers also prized expensive novelties, such as Abd ar-Rahman III's pool of mercury. To impress guests, "he would signal one of his slaves to disturb the mercury. Then there would appear in the chamber a brilliancy like lightning which would fill their hearts with fear."

Like many other medieval rulers, Abd ar-Rahman delighted in ingenious devices known as automata, among them a mechanical lion and songbirds. Mechanical songbirds also featured in a pavilion of the Baghdad caliph's palace, where they were perched in a silver and gold tree with fruits made of jewels. In the early 1200s an Iraqi author wrote and illustrated a whole book about automata, giving instructions for making all kinds of devices shaped like animals or people, including ones that played music, told the time, dispensed wine, or poured water for hand washing.

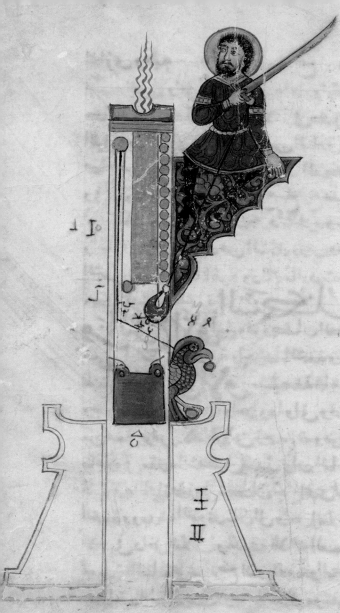

This illustration from an Iraqi book about automata shows a device that uses a candle, weights, pulleys, and a mechanical bird and swordsman to tell the time.

In medieval Muslim lands, water was a precious resource, the more so because Islam required people to wash before prayer and after such bodily activities as going to the bathroom or passing gas. Royal palaces and the mansions of high officials had the luxury of plumbing that gave them running water, indoor lavatories, and fountains and fishponds to ornament their gardens. In the Middle East people also used water to provide a form of air-conditioning by soaking pieces of heavy cloth and stretching them across windows. Wet cloth could also be put in a wooden frame hanging from the ceiling, fixed so that a servant could move it back and forth to fan the room's occupants. Another way to cool off was to soak in a *sirdab*, a sunken pool. In Samarra the royal *sirdab*s were underground and had double walls that could be packed with ice or filled with running water.

Gardens with cool fountains and shady trees also provided some escape from the heat. Courtyards and gardens were important elements in medieval Muslim palaces, offering fresh air and beauty as well as helping to keep the surrounding rooms well ventilated. Rulers sometimes filled their gardens with plants collected from other countries. The caliph al-Qahir, for example, had sour orange trees imported from India to Baghdad. Abd ar-

Rahman I grew plants from his native Syria in the gardens of Rusafa, his summer palace. Homesick, he wrote this poem about one of his date palms:

In Rusafa I came upon a palm;
here in these western lands a sight so rare,
I said: You stand alone, like me so far from home,
you miss the children and our loved ones there;
you have not grown . . . in native soil.
Like you I too must breathe the alien air.

A grand vizier,
or chief administrator,
portrayed by an
eighteenth-century
Swiss artist

THREE

The Men in Power

A monarch will not favor you unless he hopes to be
at ease while you labor and exert yourself in his service.

→→ SAMUEL HA-NAGID, ELEVENTH-CENTURY JEWISH GENERAL, VIZIER, AND POET

MEDIEVAL MUSLIM RULERS WERE GREATLY influenced by Persian ideas about royalty, government, and court life. One Persian guideline they especially kept in mind went like this: the ruler's authority was upheld by the army; the army was supported by money; money came from taxes; taxes derived from cultivation (meaning prosperity from trade and manufacturing as well as agriculture); and cultivation could only be maintained through justice, reliable officials, and good political advice. A wise ruler never forgot these connections, and filled his court with men who could help him carry out his responsibilities.

A RULER'S DAYS AND DUTIES

A group of chieftains had come to see the Fatimid caliph al-Muizz at his palace. The servants showed them to a plain room that was carpeted with simple felt mats. There al-Muizz, wearing an unadorned tunic, sat cross-legged at a low writing desk, books and papers surrounding him. When he looked up from his work to greet his visitors, he said,

> Dear brothers, this morning, with such a winter cold, I said to the princes' mother . . . "What do you think—do our brothers actually suppose that on such a day as this we eat and drink, loll about on costly pillows, covered in brocade and silk, . . . smelling of musk, drinking wine and singing, as do those who have their minds on this world?" Then it occurred to me to send for you, so that you might see with your own eyes how I behave when I am alone and removed from your gaze.

Al-Muizz was a ruler who took his duties seriously, spending his day on paperwork instead of pleasure. The Abbasid caliph al-Mansur was similarly well disciplined. He rose before dawn and meditated until the official time for morning prayer. After prayer he went to the *iwan* and held audience. Like most people, he took a nap during the heat of midday. The rest of the afternoon was devoted to conversation with his family. After the evening prayer he met with his advisers and took care of his official correspondence.

A ruler's correspondence included letters to and from ambassadors, governors, and other officials. There were also intelligence reports to read, evaluate, and act on. The Abbasid caliphs had a combined postal and intelligence service called the *barid*. Its agents reported directly to the caliph, informing him of everything from changing food prices to possible disturbances of the peace. The *barid* kept an eye on governors, judges, and administrators in every city ruled by the caliph. The agents also delivered his mail.

Dealing with intelligence reports and similar matters involved only the ruler and his secretaries. But when he held audience there might be hundreds of courtiers in attendance. During the audience he received ambassadors and guests, made proclamations, appointed governors and other officials, and granted favors to courtiers. This was serious business. Al-Mansur, for example, was usually very kind to his page boys and understanding about their noisy games when they were off duty. But, he cautioned one page, "My boy, if you see I have put on my robes, or just returned from holding audience, then be sure that none of you comes near me in case I do him a mischief."

Anyone who wanted to attend an audience first had to get permission from the chamberlain, who was the head servant at the palace and organized all the audiences.

Courtiers had to be properly dressed; in Baghdad they were expected to wear black, the official color of the Abbasid court. The chamberlain admitted them to the *iwan* strictly in order of rank. Others attending the audience were sent in by group. For example, a learned singer and poet named Ishaq al-Mosuli first went in with the singers, but before another audience asked the chamberlain to let him enter with the writers and philosophers. This was granted, and then later—again at his request—he was admitted with the religious scholars. Ishaq's final triumph was to go into the audience beside the chief judge, after which the caliph granted him the privilege of accompanying him to the mosque on Fridays.

Court protocol required those admitted to the caliph's presence

A scene from the Persian epic *Shahnama* shows a ruler in an outdoor pavilion
with his warriors, courtiers, lions, and elephants.

ADVICE FOR THE IDEAL RULER

Tahir ibn Husayn, the Abbasid caliph's governor of northeastern Persia in 821, wrote a long letter to his son, the governor of Syria, about how to be a good ruler. According to ninth-century historians, the caliph was so impressed with Tahir's advice that he ordered copies of it sent to all his officials in the provinces. People of the time seemed to feel that it was a perfect expression of their ideas about good government. In the excerpts below, Tahir discusses fairness in taxation and a ruler's responsibilities to his less fortunate subjects.

Look carefully into the matter of the land-tax which the subjects have an obligation to pay. . . . Divide it among the tax payers with justice and fairness with equal treatment for all. Do not remove any part of the obligation to pay the tax from any noble person just because of his nobility or any rich person because of his richness or from any of your secretaries or personal retainers. Do not require from anyone more than he can bear, or exact more than the usual rate.

[As a ruler, you should look after] the affairs of the poor and destitute, those who are unable to bring their complaints of ill-treatment to you personally and those of wretched estate who do not know how to set about claiming their rights. . . . Turn your attention to those who have suffered injuries and their orphans and widows and provide them with allowances from the state treasury. . . . Give pensions from the state treasury to the blind. . . . Set up hospices where sick Muslims can find shelter, and appoint custodians for these places who will treat the patients with kindness and physicians who will cure their illnesses.

to kneel before him and kiss the ground. There were other gestures of respect, and specific ways courtiers were expected to word their greetings, reports, and requests. During an audience, no one was allowed to laugh, fidget, slouch, or speak until spoken to. The ruler was also expected to follow certain standards of behavior, which one royal adviser summed up this way: "Allow people access to your person as much as possible and show your face to them as often as possible. Order your guards to treat them politely, be humble with them and show them the face of your approval. When questioning them, be gentle and grant them a share of your benef-icence." This applied especially to those audiences in which the common people were allowed to come before the ruler with their complaints and problems.

Another important duty for a ruler was to protect Islam, the *umma*, his people, and their interests. There were several ways to do this, as the Umayyad caliph Mu'awiya outlined: "I never use my voice if I can use my money, never my whip if I can use my voice, never my sword if I can use my whip. But, if I have to use my sword, I will." Mu'awiya, like many others, was a ruler who did not hesitate to lead his own armies. The Middle Ages' most renowned Muslim warrior-ruler was Saladin, the sultan of Egypt and Syria. Andalusian traveler Ibn Jubayr praised his "memorable deeds in affairs of the world and of religion, his zeal in waging holy war against the enemies of God. . . . God in his mercy gave to the Muslims here this Sultan, who never retires to a place of rest, nor long abides at ease, nor ceases to make the saddle his council-chamber." Even many of the Europeans he fought during the Third Crusade admired Saladin and regarded him as a model of bravery and honor.

Rulers might wage war against other states, but at home they valued peace and order. According to Nizam al-Mulk, vizier to the

Seljuk sultan Malik-Shah, prosperity was the best road to true security. Therefore a ruler should

> bring to pass that which concerns the advance of civilization, such as constructing underground channels [aqueducts], digging main canals, building bridges across great waters, rehabilitating villages and farms, raising fortifications, building new towns, and erecting lofty buildings and magnificent dwellings; he will have inns built on the highways and schools for those who seek knowledge; for which things he will be renowned for ever.

Moreover, the ideal ruler was a man who would "close the doors of corruption, confusion and discord"—a man to whom God gave

Saladin (seated on the left) accepts the surrender of Crusaders and makes a treaty with their leader, Richard the Lionheart. This scene was painted by Syrian artist Saed Tahssin in 1954.

The Men in Power

"such dignity and majesty in the eyes and hearts of men, that under his just rule they may live their lives in constant security and ever wish for his reign to continue."

THE RULER'S RIGHT HAND

A vizier such as Nizam al-Mulk was a tremendous asset to a ruler, helping him carry out all his duties effectively. Very often it was the vizier who actually saw to the day-to-day tasks of running the realm, while the ruler tended more to the ceremonial aspects of his office. This was what the caliph Harun ar-Rashid expected. When he appointed his first vizier after coming to the throne, he told him, "I have invested you with the rule of my flock. Removing the burden from my shoulders to yours. Govern them as you think right; appoint to office whom you will and remove whom you will. Conduct all affairs as you see fit."

In the first century or so of the Abbasid caliphate, the vizier's role varied according to the individual caliph's wishes. Generally the vizier was a chief adviser and assistant to the ruler. But as government grew more complex, the vizier's position evolved, until he also became the head of the entire administration. He oversaw all the government bureaus, called *diwans*. The *diwan*s handled a variety of matters: records, correspondence, tax collection, payments to the army, pension payments, budget control, and so on. Each bureau had many subdivisions and many clerks working for it. The amount of paperwork they generated was immense. (Luckily, paper was readily available—the technique of making paper out of cloth rags came to the Muslim world from China in the eighth century. The new writing material was plentiful and cheap by the ninth century, replacing the more expensive and more difficult-to-use papyrus and parchment that had been employed earlier.)

Another duty of the vizier was to nominate men to fill offices in the provinces. The chief provincial office was that of the emir, who was usually both the governor and the military commander for the province. Among the Abbasids this was usually a short-term position, because the caliph did not want to give an emir time to build up a local following that might challenge the caliph's authority over the region. The emir generally did not have control over taxation or justice in his province—these matters were handled by other provincial officials. Emirs were often members of the royal family, relatives of the vizier, friends of people in high places, or important political or military supporters. In the outlying provinces, though, local ruling families might be allowed to continue to govern on the caliph's behalf.

Tahir ibn Husayn, an Abbasid emir who came from a prominent

The emir of Córdoba gives instructions to officials in his government.

Persian family, made this recommendation for handling government bureaucracy:

> Keep an eye on the officials at your court and on your secretaries. Give them each a fixed time each day when they can bring you their official correspondence and any documents requiring the ruler's signature. They can let you know about the needs of the various officials and about all the affairs of the provinces you rule over. Then devote all your faculties, ears, eyes, understanding and intellect, to the business they set before you: consider it and think about it repeatedly. Finally take those actions which seem to be in accordance with good judgment and justice.

Like Tahir, a number of Abbasid officials were of Persian rather than Arabian descent. In many government administrations, positions were open to men from diverse backgrounds, including non-Muslims. Some Christians and Jews were able to rise to high ranks. For example, several Christians held the office of vizier for Egypt's Fatimid caliphs. A Jew, Samuel ha-Nagid, was vizier and chief military commander for an eleventh-century ruler of Granada. During this period, when al-Andalus had broken up into a number of warring kingdoms, Samuel won victory after victory, successfully defending Granada's borders for the almost twenty years he led the army.

POETS AND SCHOLARS

Like many other courtiers and officials, Samuel ha-Nagid was also a poet, and even rulers wrote poetry from time to time. Poetry was an important part of court culture, and people in high places were usually eager to lend their support to poets and welcome them to court. For example, Mahmud of Ghazni was the patron of the poet Firdawsi, author of the great Persian epic *Shahnama (Book of Kings)*, which told the stories of Persia's legendary kings and heroes. The *Shahnama* became one of the most popular books in the eastern part of the Muslim world, and episodes from it inspired numerous works of art.

The vizier Nizam al-Mulk extended his help to another famous Persian poet, Omar Khayyam. The two were old friends; as boys they had pledged that if one of them rose to high office as an adult, he would grant any favor he could to the other. When the time came, Omar's request was modest: "Let me live in a corner under the shadow of your fortune, to spread wide the advantages of Science, and pray for your long life and prosperity." Nizam al-Mulk awarded his old friend a generous pension, and Omar spent the rest of his days "in winning knowledge of every kind, and especially in Astronomy, wherein he attained to a very high pre-eminence. Under the Sultanate of Malik-Shah, he . . . obtained great praise for his proficiency in science, and the Sultan showered favors upon him."

Today Omar Khayyam is best known for his collection of verses *Rubaiyat*, but he was also a superb astronomer and mathematician.

Omar Khayyam working on mathematical and astronomical problems, as pictured by a modern artist

Along with poets, many scientists and scholars found favor with medieval Muslim rulers. The Abbasid caliph al-Mamun, for instance, patronized al-Khwarizmi (whose name is the source of our word *algorithm*), the great mathematician who developed algebra—which gets its name from the second word in the title of his book *Hisab al-Jabr wa 'l-Muqabala (The Compendious Book on Calculation by Completion and Balancing)*. Al-Mamun was also one of many upper-class Muslims who supported the translation of ancient Greek philosophical and scientific texts. A great number of these had been lost in western Europe after the fall of Rome in the fifth century. The Arabic translations would eventually play a crucial role in reintroducing Europeans to many works of Plato, Aristotle, Euclid, and others.

Some of the learned men who were most prominent at court were physicians. Abu al-Qasim, sometimes known as Albucasis (936–1013), worked in al-Zahra as physician to the caliph. Abu al-Qasim's writings included medical books that explained surgical procedures in great detail. Avicenna, or Ibn Sina (980–1037), worked for various emirs and sultans in Persia and what is now Uzbekistan. He wrote more than four hundred books, on many subjects but most notably on medicine. His multivolume encyclopedia, *Canon of Medicine*, was translated into Latin in the twelfth century, as were some of Abu al-Qasim's works. These translations became the standard medical texts for European doctors and surgeons for almost six hundred years.

Another renowned scholar-doctor was Ibn Rushd, commonly known as Averroës (pronounced

A fourteenth-century Italian artist painted this portrait of Averroës, whose philosophical thought was admired in Christian Europe as well as in the Muslim world.

ah-VAIR-oh-eez; 1126–1198). He was the personal physician to one of the caliphs of al-Andalus and eventually became vizier as well. He studied not only medicine but also astronomy, law, politics, religion, and philosophy. He wrote important commentaries on Aristotle and Plato, and worked to harmonize the logical thought of ancient Greek philosophy with the religion of Islam. In the twelfth century Averroës's commentaries were translated into Latin and became a major influence on medieval Christian thought. A physician and philosopher of equal standing was Maimonides (*my-MAH-ni-deez*; 1135–1204), or Moses ben Maimon. Originally from Córdoba, he spent much of his life in Cairo, where he was both a leader of the Jewish community and physician to Saladin's family and vizier. Maimonides's great work *A Guide for the Perplexed* sought to harmonize Greek philosophy with Judaism. Maimonides also wrote significant works on Jewish law and belief, and his writings have played a role in Jewish thought ever since.

Maimonides, pictured here by an eighteenth-century artist, is still honored as one of Judaism's greatest philosophers.

An aristocratic woman closes her book so that she can give her attention to her daughter as they enjoy spending time together in a garden. This miniature painting was probably made in Afghanistan during the 1400s.

FOUR

Royal Women

I am, by God, fit for high positions,
And am going my way, with pride!
→ WALLADAH BINT AL-MUSTAKFI,
ELEVENTH-CENTURY ANDALUSIAN PRINCESS AND POET

MONG THE UPPER CLASSES OF THE MEDIEVAL Muslim world, men and women lived in almost separate realms. Court, the military, and government administration were for men. Women's primary concerns, as in most premodern societies, were supposed to be pleasing their husbands and bearing and raising children. The men's world was public, the women's private. Because of the well-guarded privacy in which most women lived, we don't know as many details about their lives as we would like. But what we do know shows that palace women often interacted with the public sphere, contributing to their society and influencing events in important ways.

THE *HURAM*

In Muslim households, the harem was the part of the home that was private, only for the family. It was where the family's women would stay when men they were not related to were visiting. Providing this safe place was part of a man's duty to protect his wife and children. In a poor household, the harem might be only a screened-off corner—but where a ruler was concerned, the harem could be an entire palace building. The term *harem*, however, does not seem to have been used much by medieval authors discussing the women of a royal household. It was more common to refer to the ruler's *huram*, the group of people, particularly women, that were under his protection. Part of the reason for this was probably that during the early Abbasid caliphate the members of the *huram* did not have one designated place to live. Rather, royal women tended to have their own palaces and households in Baghdad, just as nonruling male members of the royal family did. By the late ninth century, though, the caliph's palace had a separate, secluded women's quarters for the *huram*, and this set the pattern for palace harems throughout the Muslim world.

It is hard to tell how many women belonged to the *huram* at any one time; it was said that the caliph Harun ar-Rashid had more than two thousand women under his protection. Muslim law entitled a man to have up to four legal wives, so long as he could provide equally for each of them. Rulers and very wealthy men could also afford to buy slaves, and favorite slave women often became unofficial wives to their owners. Most harem women, though, were probably servants and entertainers.

Some rulers, such as Harun ar-Rashid (like his father before him) made special efforts to seek out and buy beautiful singers and musicians to join their *huram*. Even though they were slaves, for

many young women this was a golden opportunity, the only one they might have to use their talents and gain an education. They might also become very wealthy, thanks to gifts from the ruler and his friends. Many medieval Muslim authors told of singing girls who were exceptionally intelligent, clever, and generous, who could improvise poetry, memorize hundreds of songs, discuss history and literature, and recite from the Qur'an. These gifted women did

Women talk, drink tea, play music, sew, and look after children in the harem of a wealthy Syrian home.

much to create the atmosphere of refined culture that distinguished many courts.

Some women entered the harem after being captured during warfare; for example, at various times there were many women from the Byzantine Empire in Muslim rulers' harems. Aristocratic women from outlying regions of Persia and Afghanistan sometimes became part of the Abbasid *huram* in order to strengthen the caliph's connections with those distant, often unruly parts of his realm. It also became common for women from Turkish lands to join the harem, just as men from those lands were recruited as Mamluks, or slave-soldiers. And sometimes a ruler or other powerful man would take a widow or divorced woman into his *huram* as a way of giving her protection that she otherwise would not have.

How did women of the *huram* spend their time? Musicians and singers would have to practice, of course, and servants always had work to do. Women could entertain themselves and one another with stories and dance. Those who could read might study the Qur'an or enjoy the *Shahnama* and other literary works. Some wrote poetry and songs of their own. Some practiced calligraphy, the art of elegant writing. We read of others who were perfume makers, and of one who was an architect and designed a new pavilion for the Samarra palace complex. The wealthiest women—the ruler's mother, wives, daughters, and favorite slaves—had business deals, investments, real estate interests, and charitable donations to look after, which they did with the help of their own staffs of secretaries and messengers. And of course many women would spend much of their time taking care of their children.

POWER BEHIND THE SCENES

As Averroës wrote, women's activities were largely limited to "the business of procreation, rearing and breast-feeding." But Averroës

PRINCESS POETS

Since poetry was such an important part of court life, it is not surprising to learn that many royal women composed poetry. We know the names of a number of these poets, among them Maisuna, daughter of a Bedouin chief and wife of the first Umayyad caliph; Ulayya bint al-Mahdi, a half sister of Harun ar-Rashid; and Walladah bint al-Mustakfi, daughter of the last caliph of Córdoba. Unfortunately, few of their writings have been preserved. Ulayya bint al-Mahdi's poems are difficult or impossible to find, and we have only one poem by Maisuna. In it she expresses a longing to return to her desert tribe, leaving court and her royal husband:

> The russet suit of camel's hair,
> With spirits light, and eye serene,
> Is dearer to my bosom far
> Than all the trappings of a queen.
>
> The humble tent and murmuring breeze
> That whistles thro' its fluttering wall,
> My unaspiring fancy please
> Better than towers and splendid halls. . . .
>
> The rustic youth unspoilt by art,
> Son of my kindred, poor but free,
> Will ever to Maisuna's heart
> Be dearer, pamper'd fool, than thee.

The existing poems by Walladah (ca. 1001–1080) were preserved by historians, who also wrote about her independence (she never married), her gatherings of poets and musicians, and her romance with the poet Ibn Zaydun, to whom she wrote these lines:

> I wonder; is there no way for us to meet again
> After this separation, and tell again each other of our love?
>
> Before, when you visited me during the winter season,
> I spurned the brazier, so great was my fire of passion!
>
> Time passes, yet I see no end to your long absence,
> Nor does patience free me from the bondage of yearning!
>
> May God pour rain on the land where you're dwelling
> From every cloud, in mighty streams, to freshen it!

also thought, "it is not impossible that there may be among them philosophers and rulers." Nizam al-Mulk, on the other hand, was quite certain that women "have not complete intelligence." He recommended that women should not be allowed to involve themselves in politics at all. And ruling, he felt, was out of the question: God had put men over women, and "if anyone places women over men, whatever mistakes and mischiefs occur are his fault, for permitting such a thing and changing the custom."

Nizam al-Mulk's opinion was a common one in the medieval world, but he also had personal reasons for not wanting women to play any role in politics: Turkhan, wife of the Seljuk sultan whom Nizam served, did not like Nizam and was trying to get her husband to replace him as vizier with a man of her own choosing. Royal wives could often wield great influence in government matters. For instance, Harun ar-Rashid relied on the advice and support of his wife Zubayda, especially in the early years of his reign, when he was somewhat lacking in self-confidence. There was also a great deal of affection between Harun and Zubayda, and she accompanied him on at least five of his pilgrimages to Mecca. She became famous for her good works, which focused on easing the journey for poor pilgrims. Among other things, she had a wide road built across the desert from Iraq to Mecca, with wells and caravanserais all along the way, and funded construction of an aqueduct to improve the holy city's water supply.

Rulers' mothers could be even more powerful than their wives. As wife of the caliph al-Mahdi, Khayzuran was frequently appealed to by those who wanted her to influence her husband on their behalf. After her son al-Hadi came to the throne, government officials and army commanders regularly consulted with her. Al-Hadi resented this, complaining to his chief officers, "What business have

women discussing men's affairs?" and ordering his courtiers to stop going to his mother for advice and favors. When al-Hadi died, Khayzuran worked with the vizier to secure the throne for Harun ar-Rashid, her other (and favorite) son. Khayzuran was then able to resume her behind-the-scenes role in government, which she continued for the remaining three years of her life.

After Harun's reign, it became rare for Abbasid caliphs to marry, and the mothers of their successors were usually slaves. A harem slave who became the mother of a child, especially of a son, rose to a position of high rank and honor. That position was even higher if her son became caliph. Shaghab, mother of the young caliph Muqtadir, came to be known as Sayyida, "Mistress," because her role was such a dominant one. She had her own female court and courtiers, headed by a stewardess who, among other tasks, conveyed the Mistress's wishes to the vizier, generals, judges, and other officials.

Zubayda and other women benefactors helped make the journey to Mecca easier for pilgrims such as these.

Royal Women

The Mistress was immensely wealthy, thanks to the land she owned and the share of tax money she and the harem received. Once when rebels attacked Baghdad, the government was nearly bankrupt, so the vizier persuaded the caliph to seek his mother's help: "Speak to the Mistress for she is a pious and virtuous woman. If she has any money that she has saved for emergencies that might threaten her or the state, then now is the moment to use it." Use it she did, and the well-paid army successfully defended Baghdad from the rebels.

Queen mothers elsewhere in the medieval Muslim world could also enjoy great power. For example, after Seyyedeh Khatun's four-year-old son became the Buyid sultan in western Persia, she ruled in all but name until her death thirty-two years later (in 1029). During this time her wise policies and skillful diplomacy protected her realm from conquest by Mahmud of Ghazni and other powerful enemies.

At least one woman ruled as sultan in her own right. Her name was Shajar al-Durr, and her story is a dramatic one. She began her palace life as a harem slave, but by 1249 she was the favorite wife of al-Salih Ayyub, sultan of Egypt. He died in November of that year, in the midst of the Sixth Crusade—just as King Louis IX of France was poised to attack Cairo. With the heir to the throne, Turan-Shah, away in northern Iraq, Shajar al-Durr kept her husband's death a secret from almost everyone until she and the army commander were sure the political and military situation was stable. She held things together till Turan-Shah arrived, and the Egyptian army was able to defeat Louis's forces in February 1250 and to capture Louis himself in April. Then Turan-Shah made a fatal mistake. Instead of honoring the Mamluk soldiers of Cairo who had won this victory, he tried to replace them with his own Mamluks. The Cairo

Mamluks rebelled and killed him.

There was no clear successor to Turan-Shah, so in May 1250 Shajar al-Durr stepped into the power vacuum and became sultan herself. Her issuing of coins and the mention of her name as ruler in the weekly sermons at the mosque made her position official. She almost certainly had the support of the Cairo Mamluks, due to their loyalty to her late husband—and perhaps also partly because she was originally a Turkish slave, as most of the Mamluks were. Moreover, in the preceding months she had proved her strength and leadership ability, not once but several times.

A Mamluk horseman from about the time of Shajar al-Durr, engraved on a brass bowl with gold and silver inlay

The caliph in Baghdad, however, did not approve of a woman sultan and threatened to send one of his own men to take over. So in July, after finishing negotiations with Louis and getting the French out of Egypt, Shajar al-Durr stepped down in favor of her new husband, Aybak. But in fact, Shajar remained in control. As one historian of the time noted, "She dominated him, and he had nothing to say." It all came to an end, though, in 1257, when she learned Aybak was planning to take a new chief wife. Rather than lose her position, she had Aybak murdered, and then she was murdered in her turn by his Mamluks. It was a tragic end for a remarkable woman.

Midwives swaddle a newborn prince and hand him back to his mother, while in another room astrologers cast his horoscope.

FIVE

A Noble Upbringing

If thou desire that thy name should remain, train thy son in knowledge and wisdom.

↠SAADI SHIRAZI, THIRTEENTH-CENTURY PERSIAN POET

IN THE MEDIEVAL MUSLIM WORLD MOST PEOPLE, of whatever rank, wanted children, who were regarded as a blessing from God. Religious authorities encouraged people to welcome the birth of a son or a daughter with equal joy. Most rulers, though, were much more interested in having sons, who could be raised to be trusted emirs, supporters, and successors. Not every royal son could inherit his father's throne, of course. And unlike in most of western Europe, where the oldest son was the heir, there was no hard-and-fast rule about succession. A ruler could choose any of his sons to succeed him, and their mothers could be any of his wives or favorite slaves. He might even decide to pass the throne on to a brother instead. Other men in high places, such as viziers, were often able to pass their offices on to their sons or other male relatives, too.

BIRTH AND EARLY CHILDHOOD

Childbirth was extremely dangerous for both mother and baby, as it was throughout the premodern world. But families in Islamic countries, especially in the upper class, benefited from greater medical knowledge than what was available in most of Europe at the time. Doctors had tools and surgical experience that they could use to help with difficult births. Nevertheless, many mothers and babies did not survive.

If all went well with the birth, the baby would be welcomed with the Muslim call to prayer whispered in his or her ear. A week later there would be a feast—a splendid occasion in any court—and the father would announce the child's name. This publicly established the child's parentage and the father's responsibilities toward his offspring.

Most babies were breast-fed for two years by their mothers. Occasionally when two families were particularly close, by blood or friendship, the mothers would nurse each other's babies. The children were expected to regard each other almost as siblings and to honor that bond for the rest of their lives.

Young children were closely protected and spent most of their time with their mothers and, in many palaces, with the other women and children of the harem. When they played outside, they played in the gardens or courtyards of the palace. Toys included dolls, balls, and toy birds and animals—some of which might be mechanical. There were board games and seesaws and puppet shows and pets to enjoy, too.

Fathers and male relatives were also part of children's early years, relaxing with family in the privacy of the harem and giving children,

The Palace

especially boys, many of their early lessons. We can see the affection fathers felt for their children in this verse by Ibn Zuhr (Avenzoar):

> My chick, my pretty one,
> My little quail, my son:
> When we had to part
> I left him with my heart.

Ibn Zuhr was both physician and vizier to one of al-Andalus's caliphs, so his duties probably separated him from his family on a regular basis. His son nonetheless followed in his footsteps, becoming a doctor and a poet.

Early childhood ended at about age seven. For boys, this was often the time when they would be circumcised (although religious authorities had differing views on the appropriate age for

Many parents used animal fables to teach their children to love books at a young age. This illustration from a Syrian manuscript shows a rabbit tricking an elephant into believing that a reflection of the moon in a pond is the real thing.

A Noble Upbringing

circumcision—seven days, ten years, or at the beginning of puberty were other options). In most families, this important stage of life was marked by public celebrations, including parades. In royal families, the festivities could be magnificent. When the Fatimid caliph al-Muizz's three sons were old enough (in 962), he summoned all the circumcision-aged boys in his realm to come to court with their families for a monthlong festival. According to records kept by one of al-Muizz's advisers, between five and ten thousand boys were circumcised on each day of the festival. Every one of them received money and gifts from the caliph, who also provided rosewater and scented oils to soothe the boys after the painful procedure, and acrobats brought from India to entertain and distract them.

FROM SEVEN TO FOURTEEN

Seven was considered the "age of discernment," that is, the age when children could tell right from wrong. Now education became serious. All upper-class boys learned to read, and many of the girls did, too. The most important subjects were religious: the Qur'an, traditions about Muhammad, religious law, and so on. Poetry also occupied a primary place in medieval Muslim education. It helped teach eloquence, which was highly valued, and it was the traditional way of recording and passing on history. Even many "nonliterary" works—roughly half of Avicenna's writings, for example—were in poetic form. Additional topics of study might include philosophy, mathematics, geography, astronomy, and other sciences. Some of these subjects may not have been open to many girls, though.

Discipline could be harsh. For example, the Persian poet Saadi Shirazi told the following story, which he ended with a poem:

An illustrious scholar, who was the tutor of a royal prince, had the habit of striking him unceremoniously and treating him severely. The boy, who could no longer bear this violence, went to his father to complain. . . . [The father] called for the tutor and said: "Thou dost not permit thyself to indulge in so much cruelty towards the children of my subjects as thou inflictest upon my son. What is the reason?" He replied: "It is incumbent upon all persons in general to converse in a sedate manner and to behave in a laudable [praiseworthy] way but more especially upon padshahs [kings] because whatever they say or do is commented on by everybody. . . . It is the duty of a royal prince's tutor to train up the sons of his lord in refinement of morals. . . ."

Avicenna's *Canon of Medicine*, written around the year 1000, continued to be copied and consulted for nearly six hundred years. This copy was made in the fourteenth century.

A Noble Upbringing

In this illustration from *Kalila wa Dimna*, a jackal tries to convince a lion to give up hunting and devote himself to good works. The jackal does not seem to be enjoying much success at the moment.

He whom thou hast not punished when a child
Will not prosper when he becomes a man.
While a stick is green, thou canst bend it as thou listest [as you choose].
When it is dry, fire alone can make it straight.

Many of Saadi's stories and poems were meant to advise against foolishness and teach such virtues as justice, generosity, and modesty. A popular book that offered similar "life lessons" in an entertaining way was *Kalila wa Dimna*. This was a collection of fables from India that had been translated into Persian, and then into Arabic in the late 700s. It was one of the medieval Muslim world's most popular books and was often illustrated with "the depiction of animal images in a variety of colours and pigments, so that they delight the hearts of kings; and their enjoyment is increased by the pleasure to be had from these illustrations."

Officials and court secretaries enjoyed the book as much as kings, and teachers used it to help children master Arabic. At the same time, readers of all ages appreciated the antics of the wise, foolish, and crafty animal characters of *Kalila wa Dimna* and also learned about working with allies, overcoming enemies, and other useful lessons.

Royal children were generally taught at the palace by tutors, who were often distinguished poets and scholars. Children of courtiers and high officials might also be educated in the palace, or they would have their own at-home tutors. But not all officials had a palace or private education. Many rose from humbler backgrounds and got their learning in schools in their home cities. Some especially promising students left home in their search for the best education possible.

The future vizier Nizam al-Mulk, for example, was sent from his home to the city of Nishapur (in northeast Persia) to study with a famous scholar, whom he later remembered fondly: "His illustrious years exceeded eighty-five, and it was the universal belief that every boy who read the Koran or studied the traditions in his presence, would assuredly attain to honor and happiness. . . . Towards me he ever turned an eye of favor and kindness, and as his pupil I felt for him extreme affection and devotion, so that I passed four years in his service." Nizam al-Mulk also recalled the friends (including Omar Khayyam) he made at school and the study sessions they held together: "When I first came there, I found two other pupils of mine own age newly arrived. . . . Both were endowed with sharpness of wit and the highest natural powers; and we three formed a close friendship together. When the Imam [teacher] rose from his lectures, they used to join me, and we repeated to each other the lessons we had heard."

A Noble Upbringing

A doctor checks his patient's pulse. Physicians were highly respected in the medieval Muslim world.

AVICENNA'S EDUCATION

Learning was highly esteemed in the medieval Muslim world, but few people pursued it as passionately and successfully as Avicenna. Here is his own description of his education:

I busied myself with the study of . . . commentaries on physics and mathematics, and the doors of knowledge opened before me. Then I took up medicine. . . . Medicine is not one of the difficult sciences, and in a very short time I undoubtedly excelled in it, so that physicians of merit studied under me. I also attended the sick, and the doors of medical treatments based on experience opened before me. . . . At the same time I carried on debates and controversies in jurisprudence [law]. At this point I was sixteen years old.

Then, for a year and a half, I devoted myself to study. I resumed the study of logic and all parts of philosophy. During this time I never slept the whole night through and did nothing but study all day long. Whenever I was puzzled by a problem . . . I would go to the mosque, pray, and beg the Creator of All to reveal to me that which was hidden from me and to make easy for me that which was difficult. Then at night I would return home, put a lamp in front of me, and set to work reading and writing. . . . Thus I mastered logic, physics, and mathematics.

The Sultan of Bukhara . . . was stricken by an illness which baffled the physicians. . . . I appeared before him and joined them in treating him and distinguished myself in his service.

One day I asked his permission to go into their library, look at their books, and read the medical ones. . . . I went into a palace of many rooms, each with trunks full of books, back-to-back. In one room there were books on Arabic and poetry, in another books on jurisprudence, and similarly in each room books on a single subject. I . . . asked for those I needed . . . read these books, made use of them, and thus knew the rank of every author in his own subject. . . . When I reached the age of eighteen, I had completed the study of all these sciences.

APPROACHING ADULTHOOD

For many young men, mastering horsemanship, swordsmanship, and other military skills was an important part of preparing for adulthood.

At fourteen or fifteen, young people were considered to enter puberty. Girls would often get married at this point, although, as in some other ancient and medieval societies, they might become engaged at a younger age. The daughters of the early Abbasid caliphs were usually married to other members of the royal family, typically cousins. But there are no records of caliphs' daughters' marriages after the early 800s, so we don't know whether they continued to marry as before or if they remained unmarried and living in seclusion.

We do know that after puberty, girls were generally allowed to socialize only with their families and were not allowed in the presence of men who were not related to them. So Harun ar-Rashid's half sister, the poet Ulayya, could only sing or recite her poems at family parties. On the other hand, Harun's sister Banuqa was such a favorite with their father that he let her dress as a boy—complete with a sword at her belt—and go riding with him and his attendants.

Boys, too, could marry when they reached puberty, although they usually waited longer—and, as we have seen, most of the later Abbasid caliphs never married at all. In any case, for upper-class boys the focus of young adulthood was generally still education and training for their future place in society. This training might take the form of practical experience, as in the case of Harun ar-Rashid.

Around the age of fourteen Harun received his first military command (with the help of more experienced men): a campaign against the Byzantines in southern Anatolia. Two years later his father had him lead another foray, deeper into the Byzantine Empire this time. As a result he helped negotiate a treaty with the empress Irene, who agreed to pay the caliphate tribute for the next three years. By the age of eighteen or nineteen, Harun had been made emir of a large territory stretching from western Iraq to what is now Tunisia. His father died not long after, having left the caliphate first to Harun's older brother and then to Harun. When his brother died a year later, Harun ar-Rashid fulfilled the destiny his father had trained him for, becoming one of the Muslim world's most renowned rulers.

With trumpets, kettledrums, and flags flying, members of the caliph's guard ride in parade to mark the end of Ramadan, the month of fasting.

SIX

Pageantry, Pleasures, and Perils

Think, in this batter'd Caravanserai
Whose Doorways are alternate Night and Day,
How Sultan after Sultan with his Pomp
Abode his Hour or two, and went his way.

→→OMAR KHAYYAM, ELEVENTH-CENTURY PERSIAN SCIENTIST AND POET

LIVING AT THE TOP LEVEL OF THEIR SOCIETY, rulers and high officials enjoyed wealth, luxury, the arts, privilege, and power. Many of the best things in life were theirs—but so were many of the worst. Their exalted position often made these men objects of jealousy, suspicion, fear, hatred, and violence. Royal women, too, even secluded in the harem, could be subject to the same troubles, in addition to the frustrations that came with the limits on their own activities. And no one was entirely safe from life's routine annoyances and hardships—there were fleas and mosquitoes, disease, old age, and death in the palace as anywhere else. Yet it was the ups and downs together that made up the whole of life, and people accepted that. The court poet Rudaki captured the feelings of many in his audience when he wrote:

Happy he who gave and could take pleasure,
unhappy he who neither took nor gave.
This world is wind and cloud and mirage.
Pour more wine, for what will be, will be.

SPECIAL OCCASIONS

When we think of the pageantry surrounding medieval rulers, we tend to envision events such as coronations and royal weddings. In the Dar al-Islam, however, there were no coronations. Instead there was a ceremony in which officials, army officers, and other important individuals approached the newly proclaimed ruler (or his representative) one at a time, took his hand, and swore their loyalty. Men who gave their oath to one of the caliphs of al-Andalus were exhorted with these words:

And this is the admonition, to the caliph and to his officers and to the Muslim folk, which binds you to him and him to you, that he may not blast your deputations with fire, nor keep back from you anything that his government extends to you, that he may give you what you should receive, and not conceal himself from you. May God help you to fulfil your obligations, and help him in the charge of your affairs.

In early Abbasid times the ceremony of homage, lasting many days, was held in Baghdad's main mosque. At other times and places it was less public, with small groups of influential administrators and soldiers giving their oaths in the palace, almost in secret, and the result being announced to the rest of the people afterward.

Royal weddings, as we have seen, were uncommon. But when they occurred, they could be stunning affairs. One of the last Abbasid caliphs to marry was Harun ar-Rashid's son al-Mamun; his bride was Buran, the daughter of one of his chief political supporters. At the wedding, Harun's widow Zubayda presented Buran with a thousand pearls and a precious family heirloom, a one-hundred-year-old sleeveless jacket with rubies down its front and back. The wedding festivities lasted two weeks, during which al-Mamun gave bonuses not only to the soldiers who had accompanied him to Buran's hometown but also to the camel drivers and boatmen who had helped transport the wedding party. Lavish gifts were given to all the wedding guests, too. At one banquet, it was said, Buran's father scattered among his guests slips of paper, each with the name of an estate written on it, and each estate became the property of whoever picked up that piece of paper.

The Fatimid caliphs of Egypt liked to display their wealth and power with processions past the grand buildings of Cairo. These magnificent parades were held on as many occasions as possible, including the yearly Nile flood, the installation of high officials, and both Muslim and Christian holy days. The Mamluk sultans also

Amid the flowers of his garden, a sultan grants a favor to a kneeling woman. Her gold-embroidered garments indicate her high status, but only hint at the richness with which Abbasid royal women were clothed.

Pageantry, Pleasures, and Perils

staged grand parades through Cairo. For example, they marked the beginning of summer with a stately procession featuring the sultan and his courtiers all dressed in lightweight white robes instead of their winter robes of heavy dyed wool.

LEISURE TIME

Al-Mutadid, an eleventh-century ruler of Seville, wrote:

I divide my time between hard work and leisure,
Mornings for affairs of state, evenings for pleasure!
At night I indulge in amusements and frolics,
At noon I rule with a proud mien in my court;
Amidst my trysts I do not neglect my striving
For glory and fame: these I always plan to attain.

"Frolics" were not on every ruler's schedule. There were many who preferred to spend what free time they had in prayer and religious studies. Saladin, for instance, was famous for his seriousness and piety. Not all leaders followed such a righteous example, however. Some rulers took great pleasure in wine, and plenty of it, in spite of the fact that the Qur'an instructed Muslims not to drink alcoholic beverages. This story was told about the Abbasid caliph Mutawakkil, who reigned from 847 to 860:

A young man lifts his glass in this detail from an eleventh-century wall painting.

Mutawakkil desired that every article whereon his eye should fall on the day of a certain drinking-bout should be coloured yellow. Accordingly there was erected a dome of sandalwood covered and furnished with yellow satin, and there were set in front of him melons and yellow oranges and yellow wine in golden vessels; and only those slave-girls were admitted who were yellow [blonde] with yellow brocade gowns. The dome was erected over a . . . pond, and orders were given that saffron should be put in the channels which filled it in sufficient quantity to give the water a yellow color as it flowed through the pond.

Most rulers and officials were not as self-indulgent as Mutawakkil, but they might still enjoy evening parties featuring music, poetry, wine, and witty conversation. In fact, "wine, women, and song" were the subjects of many of the poems sung or recited at such gatherings. Here is an example by Abu Nuwas, the favorite poet of the caliph al-Amin (Harun ar-Rashid's son and successor):

Deck me with crown and diadem,
and sing me my own poems.
The wine cup is a springtime
you can touch with your fingers,
and the heat of the wine seeps slowly
from my tongue all the way to my feet.

Poems and songs were generally accompanied by five or six musicians playing flute, drum, tambourine, and stringed instruments. (All of the instruments used in the Abbasid court are still played in the Middle East today. One—the pear-shaped, guitarlike oud—made its way from al-Andalus into the rest of Europe, where it became known as the lute and remained extremely popular well into the 1700s.) Singers, musicians, and poets usually performed behind a curtain that separated them from the ruler and his companions. This was especially important when women were present, as either performers or audience members, so that they would be shielded from the view of unrelated men.

Music and poetry were also part of more public gatherings, such as banquets. Feasts were held both for holidays and for state occasions—for instance, the celebration of a military victory. The poems recited at these times would tend to be in praise of the ruler. It was a long-standing tradition in Arabic culture to glorify leaders in the most eloquent language possible, and this was one of the chief jobs of a court poet. Here are a few lines from a praise poem composed in the mid-900s by al-Mutanabbi for his patron, the emir of Damascus:

> Whether at war or at peace, you aim at the heights, whether you
>   tarry or hasten.
> Would that we were your steeds when you ride forth, and your
>   tents when you alight!
> Every day you load up afresh, and journey to glory, there to dwell.

Eating, drinking, music, and poetry were not the only forms of royal recreation. Active pursuits included polo, mock combats, and hunting—often with the help of hounds, falcons, ferrets, or cheetahs. Many animals were hunted for their meat or skins, but others were captured to be added to the menageries, or private zoos, that were part of some palaces. Among the quieter palace pastimes were card games, backgammon, and chess. Even people who loved chess sometimes found it too quiet, though. At one royal chess tournament, al-Mamun scolded the silent, concentrat-

FABULOUS FEAST FOOD

Ibrahim ibn al-Mahdi—poet, musician, and author of the first Arabic cookbook—delighted in coming up with special dishes for the banquets and dinner parties held by his nephew, the caliph al-Mamun. Ibrahim's most stunning creation was a dish made of hundreds of fish tongues put together in the shape of a giant sea creature, perfect in detail right down to its scales. Not all feast foods were so extravagant, though. Here is a recipe for *bazmaawurd*, a Persian dish that became a favorite first course at Abbasid banquets.

Ingredients:

1 large wheat tortilla or thin flatbread

1 precooked chicken breast, chopped into small pieces

2 tablespoons chopped walnuts

2 peeled, seeded, and chopped lemons

1 tablespoon finely chopped fresh tarragon or one teaspoon dried tarragon

1 tablespoon finely chopped fresh mint or one teaspoon dried mint

2 tablespoons finely chopped fresh basil or two teaspoons dried basil

Mix all the ingredients (except the flatbread) together in a bowl, then sprinkle the mixture evenly on the flatbread. Roll up the flatbread and cut it into four slices (use toothpicks, if necessary, to keep them from unrolling). Place them on a baking sheet or oven-proof plate and put them in the oven at 300° F for ten minutes, or until warm. Serve and enjoy!

Above: Dancers and musicians entertain at a royal banquet in a scene from the *Shahnama*.

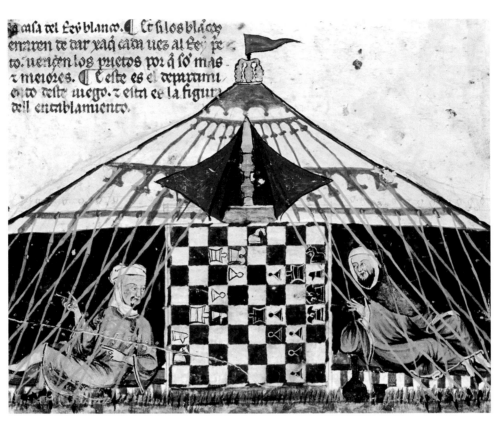

ing players and watchers, "Chess and politeness do not go well together! Talk naturally as you would among yourselves."

INTRIGUE AND WAR

The monarch has no lack of people in whom disfavour has aroused resentment, base fellows spoilt by royal favour, impatient ones who, having received double their due, suppose, in their ignorance of their true worth and their narrowminded ingratitude, that their proper share is larger and their right to it better founded than it really is. . . .

So wrote al-Jahiz, going on at still greater length to describe the malcontents and troublemakers who could cause problems for a

Soldiers in Fatimid Egypt practice fighting with staffs.

ruler. Al-Jahiz had recently lived through a much worse situation, though: a civil war between Harun ar-Rashid's two sons al-Amin and al-Mamun.

Before his death, Harun had carefully and publicly planned out the succession: al-Amin would take the throne as caliph, and al-Mamun would be his heir. Meanwhile al-Mamun was to be the virtually independent governor of a large Persian province. The two brothers signed documents promising their loyalty to each other; these documents also provided that if al-Amin broke his promises to al-Mamun, al-Mamun would become caliph immediately. But in the first year of his reign, al-Amin tried to deprive his brother of lands and income, refused to let al-Mamun's wife and children leave Baghdad to join al-Mamun in Persia, and then named his own infant son successor instead of al-Mamun. Not only was he breaking his

Pageantry, Pleasures, and Perils

sworn oath, but he had the documents recording that oath burned.

These dishonorable actions lost al-Amin the support of many of his subjects, including the influential governor of Mecca and Medina, who declared, "I have decided to renounce my allegiance to him and to swear allegiance to Ma'mun as caliph." By August 812, almost every part of the realm had done the same. But al-Amin still held Baghdad, and the two sides fought over the city for a bloody, horrible year until al-Amin was captured and killed. Meanwhile, influenced by his vizier, al-Mamun himself remained in Persia, and Baghdad continued to be torn by violence till he returned to the capital in 819.

The war between the two brothers was one of the worst conflicts in the Muslim community. Many people blamed it, in part, on the viziers who guided the royal brothers' policies, as one poet mourned:

> Have you seen the kings, what they did
> When nobody restrained them with good advice?
> How would it have harmed them if they kept to their pact . . .
> If they had not competed to shed the blood of their supporters
> And sent out warriors to fight against each other . . . ?

The influence wielded by viziers and other powerful courtiers could indeed be immense. Many officials did use their position to advance their own interests and increase their own wealth by dishonorable, dishonest means. But it wasn't always a matter of an adviser manipulating the ruler he was supposed to serve; sometimes the ruler willingly gave his vizier the power to make decisions and plans for him.

Sometimes, too, a ruler turned against his officials and courtiers. Harun ar-Rashid ordered the imprisonment, and execution in one case, of the father and sons who had long served him loyally as viziers, governors, and in other offices. No one at the time was quite sure why (nor are modern historians), but all kinds of explanations were given, many having to do with jealousy and conspiracy and similar intrigues. What is clear—from this episode and from other stories of disgrace and assassination in high places—is that no one was ever completely secure in their position.

Security was uncertain not only for individuals but for entire dynasties and states, as we have seen already. Worst of all, though, were the times when the *umma* itself was in danger. Christian conquests in al-Andalus, Sicily, and Syria in the eleventh century all seemed such a threat—although some people were more worried about it than others. When cru- saders captured Jerusalem in 1099, neither the Seljuk sultans nor the caliphs were much inter- ested in taking action, leading the chief judge of Baghdad to exclaim to the caliph and his court, "How dare you slumber in the shade of complacent safety, leading lives as frivolous as garden flowers, while your brothers in Syria have no dwelling place save the saddles of camels and the bellies of vul- tures?" It was left to Saladin and other Muslim leaders in Egypt and Syria to recover the territories that had fallen to the crusaders.

Even more feared than the crusaders were the Mongols, originally from the region north

Neither mountains nor any other barrier could stop the advance of the Mongols.

of China. Fierce, well-organized, highly mobile warriors, they began attacking the eastern edge of the Muslim world in 1219. By 1221 they were overrunning Persia. An Iraqi historian of the time, Ibn al-Athir, wrote that the Mongols "in just one year seized the most populous, the most beautiful, and the best cultivated part of the earth whose characters excelled in civilization and urbanity. In the countries which have not yet been overrun by them, everyone spends the night afraid they may appear there too." Men, women, and children were killed; mosques were vandalized and Qur'ans were burned; centers of learning were destroyed; cities and villages were repeatedly pillaged. The attacks continued, off and on, for decades.

Then in 1258, something almost unthinkable happened: the Mongols attacked and destroyed Baghdad, and killed the caliph. To Ibn al-Athir and many others, this was "the death-blow of Islam and the Muslims." Yet two years later, the Mamluks defeated the Mongols in Syria, preventing them from expanding farther into the Dar al-Islam. And by the end of the thirteenth century, most of the Mongols themselves had become Muslims. It took longer than that for the eastern part of the Muslim world to recover from the upheavals of the Mongol invasion, but it did recover, and in some ways grew richer and stronger. Although a glorious era was over, the *umma* would continue to expand and thrive.

A Chronology of Important Dynasties and Rulers

622	Muhammad founds and leads the *umma* in Medina
632–661	Rule of the four Rightly Guided Caliphs, beginning with Abu Bakr
661–750	Umayyad dynasty of caliphs rules from Damascus, Syria
	661–680 Reign of Mu'awiya
750–945	Abbasid dynasty of caliphs rules from Baghdad and Samarra (836–892), Iraq
	754–775 Reign of al-Mansur
	786–809 Reign of Harun ar-Rashid
	813–833 Reign of al-Mamun
	833–842 Reign of al-Mu'tasim
756–1031	Umayyad dynasty rules most of Spain
	756–788 Reign of Abd ar-Rahman I
	912–961 Reign of Abd ar-Rahman III
945–1055	Buyid dynasty rules Iraq and western Persia
945–1258	Abbasid caliphs hold symbolic office but exercise no real power
909–1171	Fatimid dynasty rules North Africa
	953–975 Reign of al-Muizz, who adds Egypt to the Fatimid caliphate
977–1186	Ghaznavids rule eastern Persia, Afghanistan, and northern India
	998–1030 Reign of Mahmud of Ghazni
1055–1194	Seljuk sultans rule Iraq and Persia
	1071 Sultan Alp Arslan defeats the Byzantines, allowing Seljuk Turks to begin settling in Anatolia
	1072–1092 Reign of Malik-Shah

1171–1250	Ayyubid sultans rule Egypt and much of Syria
	1171–1193 Reign of Saladin
1232–1492	Nasrid dynasty rules Granada in southern Spain
1250–1517	Mamluks rule Egypt and Syria
1258	Mongols conquer Baghdad; end of the Abbasid caliphate

Glossary

al-Andalus (also called Andalusia) the part of present-day Spain and Portugal ruled by Muslims

Bedouin nomadic tribes of Arabia and neighboring regions

brocade silk fabric with raised designs woven into it; the designs were often made with gold or silver thread

caliph (Arabic *khalifa*) the political and spiritual leader of the Muslim community, ruling as Muhammad's successor and deputy

caravanserai (Persian *karvansarai*) an inn built around a large open courtyard where caravans could rest

Crusades a series of Western European military expeditions, conducted from 1096 to 1270, to recapture Palestine from the Muslims and return it to Christian rule. The Crusaders won some battles and established a kingdom along the eastern shore of the Mediterranean Sea, but their victories were short-lived and had little permanent effect.

dynasty a series of rulers, usually related by family ties

emir (Arabic *amir*, "one who gives orders") a military commander or governor or prince, theoretically subject to the caliph but often ruling in his own right

garrison an army base

imam a man who led the prayers at the mosque; in general, a leader of the Muslim community

Mamluks slaves, usually non-Muslim Turks, bought and trained as boys or young men to become members of elite military regiments. They might also learn literary and administrative skills, which allowed them to fill government posts. After completing training, Mamluks were typically well paid for their services, and were given their freedom if they converted to Islam.

mosque (Arabic *masjid*) a Muslim house of worship

pavilion a free-standing building, often open-sided and ornamental, within a palace complex

Persia modern-day Iran

sultan (literally "authority" or "power") the Arabic term for a monarch or king, synonymous with Turkish *khan* and Persian *shah*. *Sultan* eventually became the most common title for a Muslim ruler.

Syria during the medieval period often used as the common name for the eastern Mediterranean coastal region, including Palestine and the modern countries of Lebanon, Syria, and Israel

Turks members of a variety of Turkish-speaking nomadic tribes from Central Asia; eventually they would become the dominant people in Anatolia, which as a result is now known as Turkey

umma the community of Muslims

vizier (Arabic *wazir*) a chief administrator appointed by the ruler and under his direct authority

For Further Reading

Barber, Nicola. *Everyday Life in the Ancient Arab and Islamic World.* North Mankato, MN: Smart Apple Media, 2006.

Colombo, Monica. *The Islamic World: From Its Origins to the 16th Century.* Translated by Pamela Swinglehurst. Austin, TX: Raintree Steck-Vaughn, 1994.

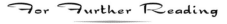

Doak, Robin. *Empire of the Islamic World.* New York: Facts on File, 2005.

Dunn, John. *The Spread of Islam.* San Diego: Lucent Books, 1996.

George, Linda S. *The Golden Age of Islam.* New York: Benchmark Books, 1998.

Nicolle, David. *Historical Atlas of the Islamic World.* New York: Checkmark Books, 2003.

Worth, Richard. *Saladin: Sultan of Egypt and Syria.* Berkeley Heights, NJ: Enslow, 2007.

Online Information

Abaza, Ismail. "Saladin (Salah al-Din Yusuf Ibn Ayyub) and His Cairo."
http://www.touregypt.net/featurestories/saladin.htm

Academic Technology Services PLACE. *Princeton Online Arabic Poetry.*
http://www.princeton.edu/~arabic/poetry/

Bartel, Nick. *Medieval Islamic Cultures.*
http://www.sfusd.k12.ca.us/schwww/sch618/Islam_New_Main.html

Foundation for Science Technology and Civilisation. *Muslim Heritage.*
http://www.muslimheritage.com

Lamprière, Denyse. "Madinat al-Zahra: Dream City."
http://www.andalucia.com/magazine/english/ed4/madinat.htm

Perry, Charles. "Cooking with the Caliphs."
http://saudiaramcoworld.com/issue/200604/cooking.with.the.caliphs.htm

Shahnama Project
http://shahnama.caret.cam.ac.uk/shahnama

Selected Bibliography

Arberry, A. J. *Moorish Poetry: A Translation of "The Pennants," An Anthology Compiled in 1243 by the Andalusian Ibn Sa'id.* Miami, FL: Granger Books, 1953.

Brett, Michael. *The Moors: Islam in the West.* London: Orbis Publishing, 1980.

Editors of Time-Life Books. *What Life Was Like in the Lands of the Prophet: Islamic World AD 570–1405.* Alexandria, VA: Time-Life Books, 1999.

Esposito, John L. *Islam: The Straight Path.* 3rd edition. New York: Oxford University Press, 1998.

Fitzgerald, Edward, ed. and trans. *Rubaiyat of Omar Khayyam, The Astronomer-Poet of Persia.* First edition (1859). Online at http://www.gutenberg.org/etext/246

Fletcher, Richard. *Moorish Spain.* New York: Henry Holt, 1992.

Irwin, Robert. *Islamic Art in Context: Art, Architecture, and the Literary World.* New York: Harry N. Abrams, 1997.

Kennedy, Hugh. *When Baghdad Ruled the Muslim World: The Rise and Fall of Islam's Greatest Dynasty.* Cambridge, MA: Da Capo Press, 2005.

Lapidus, Ira M. *A History of Islamic Societies.* Cambridge: Cambridge University Press, 1988.

Lewis, Bernard, trans. *Music of a Distant Drum: Classical Arabic, Persian, Turkish, and Hebrew Poems.* Princeton, NJ: Princeton University Press, 2001.

Lindsay, James E. *Daily Life in the Medieval Islamic World.* Westport, CT: Greenwood Press, 2005.

Lowney, Chris. *A Vanished World: Muslims, Christians, and Jews in Medieval Spain.* New York: Oxford University Press, 2006.

McNeill, William H., and Marilyn Robinson Waldman, eds. *The Islamic World* (Readings in World History, vol. 6). New York: Oxford University Press, 1973.

Robinson, Francis, ed. *The Cambridge Illustrated History of the Islamic World.* Cambridge: Cambridge University Press, 1996.

Ruthven, Malise, with Azim Nanji. *Historical Atlas of Islam.* Cambridge, MA: Harvard University Press, 2004.

Shabbas, Audrey, ed. *A Medieval Banquet in the Alhambra Palace.* Rev. ed. Berkeley, CA: AWAIR: Arab World and Islamic Resources and School Services, 1993.

Sources for Quotations

Chapter 1

p. 13 "In every age": Lindsay, *Daily Life in the Medieval Islamic World*, p. 20.

p. 17 "The Turk will hit": McNeill and Waldman, *The Islamic World*, pp. 113–115.

p. 18 "could only see": Lowney, *A Vanished World*, p. 65.

p. 18 "inspired with awe": ibid., p. 64.

p. 18 "Prophecy and the caliphate": Robinson, *The Cambridge Illustrated History of the Islamic World*, p. 33.

p. 20 "I have seen": ibid., p. 39.

Chapter 2

p. 23 "I saw a series": Irwin, *Islamic Art in Context*, p. 115.

p. 23 "Kings and princes": ibid., p. 106.

p. 24 "was the crown": Kennedy, *When Baghdad Ruled the Muslim World*, p. 136.

p. 26 "The caliph Mutawwakil": ibid., pp. 147–148.

p. 27 "had eight openings": Editors of Time-Life, *What Life Was Like in the Lands of the Prophet*, p. 81.

p. 27 "with spears": Lowney, *A Vanished World*, p. 69.

p. 28 "The fear": Editors of Time-Life, *What Life Was Like in the Lands of the Prophet*, p. 81.

The Palace

p. 30 "Three of its sides": Irwin, *Islamic Art in Context*, p. 115.

p. 33 "The water in the basin": ibid., p. 54.

p. 33 "he would signal": Editors of Time-Life, *What Life Was Like in the Lands of the Prophet*, p. 81.

p. 35 "In Rusafa": Robinson, *The Cambridge Illustrated History of the Islamic World*, p. 26.

Chapter 3

p. 37 "A monarch will not": Lowney, *A Vanished World*, p. 97.

p. 38 "Dear brothers": Editors of Time-Life, *What Life Was Like in the Lands of the Prophet*, p. 85.

p. 39 "My boy": Kennedy, *When Baghdad Ruled the Muslim World*, p. 14.

p. 41 "Look carefully": ibid., p. 204.

p. 41 "the affairs of the poor": ibid., pp. 204–205.

p. 42 "Allow people access": ibid., p. 205.

p. 42 "I never use": Editors of Time-Life, *What Life Was Like in the Lands of the Prophet*, p. 42.

p. 42 "memorable deeds": Robinson, *The Cambridge Illustrated History of the Islamic World*, p. 45.

p. 43 "bring to pass": Irwin, *Islamic Art in Context*, p. 74.

p. 43 "close the doors": Lindsay, *Daily Life in the Medieval Islamic World*, p. 20.

p. 44 "such dignity": ibid., p. 20.

p. 44 "I have invested": Kennedy, *When Baghdad Ruled the Muslim World*, p. 63.

p. 46 "Keep an eye": ibid., p. 205.

p. 47 "Let me live" and "in winning knowledge": Fitzgerald, *Rubaiyat of Omar Khayyam*, Introduction.

Chapter 4

p. 51 "I am, by God": Shabbas, *A Medieval Banquet in the Alhambra Palace*, p. 145.

p. 54 "the business of procreation": Lowney, *A Vanished World*, p. 170.

Sources for Quotations

p. 55 "The russet suit": *Medieval Sourcebook: The Poets of Arabia, Selections*, http://www.fordham.edu/halsall/source/arabianpoets1.html

p. 55 "I wonder": Shabbas, *A Medieval Banquet in the Alhambra Palace*, p. 146.

p. 56 "it is not impossible": Lowney, *A Vanished World*, p. 170.

p. 56 "have not complete" and "if anyone places": Lindsay, *Daily Life in the Medieval Islamic World*, p. 21.

p. 56 "What business": Kennedy, *When Baghdad Ruled the Muslim World*, p. 61.

p. 58 "Speak to the Mistress": ibid., p. 195.

p. 59 "She dominated": "Biographies: Female Heroes from the Time of the Crusades," http://www.womeninworldhistory.com/heroine1.html

Chapter 5

p. 61 "If thou desire": *The Bostan of Saadi*, p. 57, PDF accessed from http://www.iranchamber.com/literature/saadi/saadi.php

p. 63 "My chick": Arberry, *Moorish Poetry*, p. 8.

p. 65 "An illustrious scholar": *The Golestan of Saadi*, p. 155, PDF accessed from http://www.iranchamber.com/literature/saadi/saadi.php

p. 66 "the depiction": Irwin, *Islamic Art in Context*, p. 185.

p. 67 "His illustrious" and "When I first came there": Fitzgerald, *Rubaiyat of Omar Khayyam*, Introduction.

p. 69 "I busied myself": Esposito, *Islam: The Straight Path*, p. 54.

Chapter 6

p. 73 "Think, in this batter'd": Fitzgerald, *Rubaiyat of Omar Khayyam*.

p. 74 "Happy he": Lewis, *Music of a Distant Drum*, p. 93.

p. 74 "And this is the admonition": Brett, *The Moors*, p. 54.

p. 76 "I divide my time": Fletcher, *Moorish Spain*, p. 90.

p. 76 "Mutawakkil desired": McNeill and Waldman, *The Islamic World*, p. 102.

p. 77 "Deck me with crown": Lewis, *Music of a Distant Drum*, p. 58.

p. 78 "Whether at war": McNeill and Waldman, *The Islamic World*, p. 172.

p. 79 Recipe adapted from Charles Perry, "Cooking with the Caliphs,"

http://saudiaramcoworld.com/issue/200604/cooking.with.the.caliphs.htm

p. 80 "Chess and politeness": Editors of Time-Life, *What Life Was Like in the Lands of the Prophet*, p. 64.

p. 80 "The monarch has no lack": McNeill and Waldman, *The Islamic World*, p. 111.

p. 82 "I have decided": Kennedy, *When Baghdad Ruled the Muslim World*, p.101.

p. 82 "Have you seen": ibid., p. 105.

p. 83 "How dare you": Robinson, *The Cambridge Illustrated History of the Islamic World*, p. 43.

p. 84 "in just one year": ibid., p. 47.

p. 84 "the death-blow": McNeill and Waldman, *The Islamic World*, p. 249.

Index

Index

About the Author

KATHRYN HINDS grew up near Rochester, New York. She studied music and writing at Barnard College, and went on to do graduate work in comparative literature and medieval studies at the City University of New York. She has written more than thirty books for young people, including the books in the series LIFE IN ELIZABETHAN ENGLAND, LIFE IN ANCIENT EGYPT, LIFE IN THE ROMAN EMPIRE, LIFE IN THE RENAISSANCE, and LIFE IN THE MIDDLE AGES. Kathryn lives in the north Georgia mountains with her husband, their son, and an assortment of cats and dogs. In addition to writing, she is a teacher and performer of Middle Eastern dance and music, which she has been studying for twenty years. She is always learning more. Visit Kathryn online at http://www.kathrynhinds.com

About Our Consultant

DR. JOSEF W. (YOUSEF) MERI, Fellow and Special Scholar in Residence at the Royal Aal al-Bayt Institute for Islamic Thought in Amman, Jordan, has also been a visiting scholar at the American Research Centre in Egypt; the Hebrew University of Jerusalem; L'Institut Français d'Études Arabes in Damascus; the Near Eastern Studies Department at the University of California, Berkeley; and the Institute of Ismaili Studies, London. He earned his doctorate at Oxford University, specializing in medieval Islamic history and religion and in the history and culture of the Jews of the Near East. He is the author or co-author of numerous journal articles, encyclopedia entries, and books, including *The Cult of Saints Among Muslims and Jews in Medieval Syria* (Oxford: Oxford University Press, 2002), and he was general editor of *Medieval Islamic Civilization: An Encyclopedia* (New York and Oxford: Routledge, 2006).